Kwanzaa Surprise

Therese Shea

NEIGHBORHOOD READERS

Rosen Classroom Books & Materials™

New York

"Do you know what day it is?"
said Dad.

"No, what day is it?" said Mark.
"You will see!" said Dad.

"We put a cloth on the table,"
said Dad.

"We put a mat on the cloth,"
said Dad.

"We put candles on the mat,"
said Dad.

"We put food on the mat,"
said Dad.

"We put a cup on the mat,"
said Dad.

"We put gifts on the table,"
said Dad.

"Now do you know what day
it is?" said Dad.

"It is the first day of Kwanzaa!"
said Mark.

"Happy Kwanzaa, Mark!"
said Dad.